THE LITTLE BOOK OF
Restorative
Justice

THE LITTLE BOOKS OF JUSTICE & PEACEBUILDING

Published titles include:

The Little Books of Justice & Peacebuilding present, in highly accessible form, key concepts and practices from the fields of restorative justice, conflict transformation, and peacebuilding. Written by leaders in these fields, they are designed for practitioners, students, and anyone interested in justice, peace, and conflict resolution.

The Little Books of Justice & Peacebuilding series is a cooperative effort between the Center for Justice and Peacebuilding of Eastern Mennonite University (Howard Zehr, Series General Editor) and publisher Good Books (Phyllis Pellman Good, Senior Editor).

THE LITTLE BOOK OF
Restorative Justice

HOWARD ZEHR

Good Books®

Intercourse, PA 17534
800/762-7171
www.GoodBooks.com

Acknowledgments

A special thanks to the many friends and colleagues who gave me feedback on this manuscript. This includes my students, former students, and colleagues at the Conflict Transformation Program where I teach. I especially want to thank Barb Toews Shenk, Jarem Sawatsky, Bonnie Price Lofton, Robert Gillette, Vernon Jantzi, Larissa Fast, and Ali Gohar for their careful attention and suggestions. Although the suggestions were not always easy to hear, and I was not able to incorporate all, the book is much better because of them.

Cover photograph by Howard Zehr.

Design by Dawn J. Ranck

THE LITTLE BOOK OF RESTORATIVE JUSTICE
Copyright © 2002 by Good Books, Intercourse, PA 17534
International Standard Book Number: 978-1-56148-376-1
Library of Congress Catalog Card Number: 2002032651

Library of Congress Cataloging-in-Publication Data

Zehr, Howard
     The little book of restorative justice / Howard Zehr.
        p.cm.
     Includes bibliographical references.
     ISBN 1-56148-376-1; 978-1-56148-376-1
     1. Restorative justice. 2. Victims of crimes. 3. Criminals—Rehabilitation.
4. Corrections—Philosophy. 5. Criminal justice, Administration of. I. Title:
Restorative justice. II. Title.

HV8688.Z44 2002
364.6'8--dc21   2002032651

Table of Contents

1.
An Overview

How should we as a society respond to wrongdoing? When a crime occurs or an injustice is done, what needs to happen? What does justice require?

For North Americans, the urgency of these questions has been intensified by the traumatic events of September 11, 2001. The debate is an old one, though, and is truly international in scope.

Whether we are concerned with crime or other offenses, the Western legal system has profoundly shaped our thinking about these issues—not only in the Western world, but in much of the rest of the world as well.

The Western legal, or criminal justice, system's approach to justice has some important strengths. Yet there is also a growing acknowledgment of this system's limits and failures. Victims, offenders, and community members often feel that justice does not adequately meet their needs. Justice professionals—judges, lawyers, prosecutors, probation and parole officers, prison staff—frequently express a sense of frustration as well. Many feel that the process of justice deepens societal wounds and conflicts rather than contributing to healing or peace.

Restorative justice is an attempt to address some of these needs and limitations. Since the 1970s, a variety of programs and approaches have emerged in thousands of

3

communities and many countries throughout the world. Often these are offered as choices within or alongside the existing legal system. Starting in 1989, however, New Zealand has made restorative justice the hub of its entire juvenile justice system.

In many places today, restorative justice is considered a sign of hope and the direction of the future. Whether it will live up to this promise remains to be seen.

Restorative justice began as an effort to deal with burglary and other property crimes that are usually viewed (often incorrectly) as relatively minor offenses. Today, however, restorative approaches are available in some communities for the most severe forms of criminal violence: death from drunken driving, assault, rape, even murder. Building upon the experience of the Truth and Reconciliation Commission in South Africa, efforts are also being made to apply a restorative justice framework to situations of mass violence.

These approaches and practices are also spreading beyond the criminal justice system to schools, to the workplace, and to religious institutions. Some advocate the use of restorative approaches such as "circles" (a particular practice that emerged from First Nation communities in Canada) as a way to work through, resolve, and transform conflicts in general. Others pursue circles or "conferences" (an effort with roots both in New Zealand and Australia, and in facilitated victim-offender meetings) as a way to build and heal communities. Kay Pranis, a prominent restorative justice advocate, calls circles a form of participatory democracy that moves beyond simple majority rule (see pages 50-51 for a fuller explanation of circles as understood in the restorative justice field).

In societies where Western legal systems have replaced and/or suppressed traditional justice and conflict-resolution processes, restorative justice is providing a framework to reexamine and sometimes reactivate these traditions.

Although the term "restorative justice" encompasses a variety of programs and practices, at its core it is a set of principles, a philosophy, an alternate set of guiding questions. Ultimately, restorative justice provides an alternative framework for thinking about wrongdoing. I will explore that framework in the pages that follow, and look at how it could be put to use.

Why this *Little Book*?

In this **Little Book**, I do not try to make the case for restorative justice. Nor do I explore the many implications of this approach. Rather, I intend this book to be a brief description or overview—the *CliffsNotes*, if you will, of restorative justice. Although I will outline some of the programs and practices of restorative justice, my focus in this book is especially the principles or philosophy of restorative justice.

The Little Book of Restorative Justice is for those who have heard the term and are curious about what it implies. It is also for those who are involved in the field but are becoming unclear or losing track of what they are trying to do. I hope to help bring clarity about where the restorative justice "train" should be headed and, in some cases, to nudge the train back onto the track.

Such an effort is important at this time. Like all attempts at change, restorative justice has sometimes lost its way as it has developed and spread. With more and more programs being termed "restorative justice," the meaning of that phrase is sometimes diluted or confused. Under the inevitable pressures of working in the real world, restorative justice has sometimes been subtly co-opted or diverted from its principles.

The victim advocacy community has been especially concerned about this. Restorative justice claims to be victim-oriented, but is it really? All too often, victim groups fear, restorative justice efforts have been motivated mainly by a desire to work with *offenders* in a more positive way. Like the criminal system it aims to improve or replace, restorative justice may become primarily a way to deal with offenders.

Others wonder whether the field has adequately addressed offender needs and made sufficiently restorative efforts. Do restorative justice programs give adequate support to offenders to carry out their obligations and to change their patterns of behavior? Do the programs adequately address the harms that may have led offenders to become who they are? Are such programs becoming just another way to punish offenders under a new guise? And what about the community at large? Is it being adequately encouraged to be involved and to assume its obligations to victims, to offenders, and to its members in general?

Our past experience with change efforts in the justice arena warns us that sidetracks and diversions inevitably happen in spite of our best intentions. If advocates for change are unwilling to acknowledge and address these likely diversions, their efforts may end up much different than they intended. In fact, "improvements" can turn out to be worse than the conditions that they were designed to reform or replace.

One of the most important safeguards we can exert against such sidetracks is to give attention to core principles. If we are clear about principles, if we design our programs with principles in mind, if we are open to being evaluated by these principles, we are much more likely to stay on track.

Put another way, the field of restorative justice has grown so rapidly and in so many directions that it is sometimes difficult to know how to move into the future with integrity and creativity. Only a clear vision of principles and goals can provide the compass we need as we find our way along a path that is inevitably winding and unclear.

This book is an effort to articulate the restorative justice concept in straightforward terms. However, I must acknowledge certain limits to the framework I will lay out here. I am often considered one of the founding developers and advocates of this field. Even though I have tried hard to remain critical and open, I come with bias in favor of this ideal. Moreover, in spite of all efforts to the contrary, I write from my own "lens," and that is shaped by who I am: a white, middle-class male of European ancestry, a Christian, a Mennonite. This biography and these, as well as other, interests necessarily shape my voice and vision.

Even though there is somewhat of a consensus within the field about the broad outline of the principles of restorative justice, not all that follows is uncontested. What you read here is my understanding of restorative justice. It must be tested against the voices of others.

Finally, I've written this book within a North American context. The terminology, the issues raised, even the way the concept is formulated, reflect to some extent the realities of my setting. I hope that this book will be useful for others, as well, but it may require some translation for other contexts.

With this background and qualifications, then, what is "restorative justice"? So many misconceptions have grown up around the term that I find it increasingly important to first clarify what, in my view, restorative justice is *not*.

Restorative justice is *not* . . .

- *Restorative justice is not primarily about forgiveness or reconciliation.*

  Some victims and victim advocates react negatively to restorative justice because they imagine that the goal of such programs is to encourage, or even to coerce, them to forgive or reconcile with offenders.

  As we shall see, forgiveness or reconciliation is not a primary principle or focus of restorative justice. It is true that restorative justice does provide a context where either or both might happen. Indeed, some degree of forgiveness or even reconciliation does occur much more frequently than in the adversarial setting of the criminal justice system. However, this is a choice that is entirely up to the participants. There should be no pressure to choose to forgive or to seek reconciliation.

- *Restorative justice is not mediation.*

  Like mediation programs, many restorative justice programs are designed around the possibility of a facilitated meeting or an encounter between victims, offenders, and perhaps community members. However, an encounter is not always chosen or appropriate.

Moreover, restorative approaches are important even when an offender has not been apprehended or when a party is unwilling or unable to meet. So restorative approaches are not limited to an encounter.

Even when an encounter occurs, the term "mediation" is not a fitting description of what could happen. In a mediated conflict or dispute, parties are assumed to be on a level moral playing field, often with responsibilities that may need to be shared on all sides. While this sense of shared blame may be true in some criminal cases, in many cases it is not. Victims of rapes or even burglaries do not want to be known as "disputants." In fact, they may well be struggling to overcome a tendency to blame themselves.

At any rate, to participate in most restorative justice encounters, a wrongdoer must admit to some level of responsibility for the offense, and an important component of such programs is to name and acknowledge the wrongdoing. The neutral language of mediation may be misleading and even offensive in many cases.

Although the term "mediation" was adopted early on in the restorative justice field, it is increasingly being replaced by terms such as "conferencing" or "dialogue" for the reasons outlined above.

- *Restorative justice is not primarily designed to reduce recidivism or repeating offenses.*

    In an effort to gain acceptance, restorative justice programs are often promoted or evaluated as ways to decrease repeat crimes.

    There are good reasons to believe that, in fact, such programs will reduce offending. Indeed, the research thus far—centering mainly on juvenile offenders—is quite encouraging on this issue. Nevertheless, reduced recidivism is not the reason for operating restorative justice programs.

Reduced recidivism is a byproduct, but restorative justice is done first of all because it is the right thing to do. Victims' needs *should* be addressed, offenders *should* be encouraged to take responsibility, those affected by an offense *should* be involved in the process, regardless of whether offenders catch on and reduce their offending.

* ***Restorative justice is not a particular program or a blueprint.***

Various programs embody restorative justice in part or in full. However, there is no pure model that can be seen as ideal or that can be simply implemented in any community. We are still on a steep learning curve in this field. The most exciting practices that have emerged in the past years were not even imagined by those of us who began the first programs, and many more new ideas will surely emerge through dialogue and experimentation.

> Restorative justice is a *compass*, not a map.

Also, all models are to some extent culture-bound. So restorative justice should be built from the bottom up, by communities in dialogue assessing their needs and resources and applying the principles to their own situations.

Restorative justice is *not a map*, but the principles of restorative justice can be seen as a *compass* pointing a direction. At a minimum, restorative justice is an invitation for dialogue and exploration.

An Overview

- *Restorative justice is not primarily intended for comparatively minor offenses or for first-time offenders.*
  It may be easier to get community support for programs that address so-called "minor" cases. However, experience has shown that restorative approaches may have the greatest impact in more severe cases. Moreover, if the principles of restorative justice are taken seriously, the need for restorative approaches is especially clear in severe cases. The guiding questions of restorative justice (see page 38) may help to tailor justice responses in very difficult situations. Domestic violence is probably the most problematic area of application, and here great caution is advised.

- *Restorative justice is not a new or North American development.*
  The modern field of restorative justice did develop in the 1970s from case experiments in several communities with a proportionately sizable Mennonite population. Seeking to apply their faith as well as their peace perspective to the harsh world of criminal justice, Mennonites and other practitioners (in Ontario, Canada, and later in Indiana, U.S.A.) experimented with victim-offender encounters that led to programs in these communities and later became models for programs throughout the world. Restorative justice theory developed initially from these particular efforts.

  However, the movement owes a great deal to earlier movements and to a variety of cultural and religious traditions. It owes a special debt to the Native people of North America and New Zealand. The precedents and roots of restorative justice are much wider and deeper than the Mennonite-led initiatives of the 1970s. Indeed, they are as old as human history.

- **Restorative justice is neither a panacea nor necessarily a replacement for the legal system.**

  Restorative justice is by no means an answer to all situations. Nor is it clear that it should replace the legal system, even in an ideal world. Many feel that even if restorative justice could be widely implemented, some form of the Western legal system (ideally, a restoratively-oriented one) would still be needed as a backup and guardian of basic human rights. Indeed, this is the function that the youth courts play in the restorative juvenile justice system of New Zealand.

  Most restorative justice advocates agree that crime has both a public dimension and a private dimension. I believe it would be more accurate to say that crime has a societal dimension, as well as a more local and personal dimension. The legal system focuses on the public dimensions; that is, on society's interests and obligations as represented by the state. However, this emphasis downplays or ignores the personal and interpersonal aspects of crime. By putting a spotlight on and elevating the private dimensions of crime, restorative justice seeks to provide a better balance in how we experience justice.

- **Restorative justice is not necessarily an alternative to prison.**

  Western society, and especially the United States, greatly overuses prisons. If restorative justice were taken seriously, our reliance on prisons would be reduced and the nature of prisons would change significantly. However, restorative justice approaches may also be used in conjunction with, or parallel to, prison sentences. They are not necessarily an alternative to incarceration.

- *Restorative justice is not necessarily the opposite of retribution.*
  Despite my earlier writing, I no longer see restoration as the polar opposite of retribution. More on that later (see pages 58-59).

Restorative justice *is* concerned about needs and roles

The restorative justice movement originally began as an effort to rethink the needs which crimes create, as well as the roles implicit in crimes. Restorative justice advocates were concerned about needs that were not being met in the usual justice process. They also believed that the prevailing understanding of legitimate participants or stakeholders in justice was too restrictive.

Restorative justice expands the circle of stakeholders— those with a stake or standing in the event or the case— beyond just the government and the offender to include victims and community members also.[1]

Because this view of needs and roles was at the origin of the movement, and because the needs/roles framework is so basic to the concept, it is important to start this review there. As the field has developed, stakeholder analysis has become more complex and encompassing. The following discussion is limited to some of the core concerns that were present at the beginning of the movement and that continue to play a central role. It is also limited to "judicial" needs—those needs of victims, offenders, and community members that might be met, at least partially, through the justice system.

Victims

Of special concern to restorative justice are the needs of crime victims that are not being adequately met by the criminal justice system. Victims often feel ignored, neglected, or even abused by the justice process. This results in part from the legal definition of crime, which does not include victims. Crime is defined as against the state, so the state takes the place of the victims. Yet victims often have a number of specific needs from the justice process.

Due to the legal definition of crime and the nature of the criminal justice process, the following four types of needs seem to be especially neglected:

1. **Information.** Victims need answers to questions they have about the offense—why it happened and what has happened since. They need *real* information, not speculation or the legally constrained information that comes from a trial or plea agreement. Securing real information usually requires direct or indirect access to offenders who hold this information.
2. **Truth-telling.** An important element in healing or transcending the experience of crime is an opportunity to tell the story of what happened. Indeed, it is often important for a victim to be able to retell this many times. There are good therapeutic reasons for this. Part of the trauma of crime is the way it upsets our views of ourselves and our world, our life-stories.

Transcendence of these experiences means "re-storying" our lives by telling the stories in significant settings, often where they can receive public acknowledgment. Often, too, it is important for victims to tell their stories to the ones who caused the harm and to have them understand the impact of their actions.

3. **Empowerment**. Victims often feel like control has been taken away from them by the offenses they've experienced—control over their properties, their bodies, their emotions, their dreams. Involvement in their own cases as they go through the justice process can be an important way to return a sense of empowerment to them.

4. **Restitution or vindication.** Restitution by offenders is often important to victims, sometimes because of the actual losses, but just as importantly, because of the symbolic recognition restitution implies. When an offender makes an effort to make right the harm, even if only partially, it is a way of saying "I am taking responsibility, and you are not to blame."

Restitution, in fact, is a symptom or sign of a more basic need, the need for vindication. While the concept of vindication is beyond the scope of this booklet, I am convinced that it is a basic need that we all have when we are treated unjustly. Restitution is one of a number of ways of meeting this need to even the score. Apology may also contribute to this need to have one's harm recognized.

The theory and practice of restorative justice have emerged from and been profoundly shaped by an effort to take these needs of victims seriously.

Offenders

A second major area of concern that gave rise to restorative justice is offender accountability.

The criminal justice system is concerned about holding offenders accountable, but that means making sure offenders get the punishment they deserve. Little in the process encourages offenders to understand the consequences of their actions or to empathize with victims. On the contrary, the adversarial game requires offenders to look out for themselves. Offenders are discouraged from acknowledging their responsibility and are given little opportunity to act on this responsibility in concrete ways.

The neutralizing strategies—the stereotypes and rationalizations that offenders often use to distance themselves from the people they hurt—are never challenged. Unfortunately, then, an offender's sense of alienation from society is only heightened by the legal process and by the prison experience. For a variety of reasons the legal process tends to discourage responsibility and empathy on the part of offenders.

Restorative justice has brought an awareness of the limits and negative byproducts of punishment. Beyond that, however, it has argued that punishment is not real accountability. Real accountability involves facing up to what one has done. It means encouraging offenders to understand the impact of their behavior—the harms they have done—and urging them to take steps to put things right as much as possible. This accountability, it is argued, is better for victims, better for society, and better for offenders.

Offenders have other needs beyond their responsibilities to victims and communities. If we expect them to assume their responsibilities, to change their behavior, to become contributing members of our communities, their needs, says restorative justice, must be addressed as well. That subject is beyond the scope of this little book, but the following suggests some of what is needed:

Offenders need from justice:

1. **Accountability that**
   - addresses the resulting harms,
   - encourages empathy and responsibility,
   - and transforms shame.[2]

2. **Encouragement to experience personal transformation, including**
   - healing for the harms that contributed to their offending behavior,
   - opportunities for treatment for addictions and/or other problems,
   - enhancement of personal competencies.

3. **Encouragement and support for integration into the community.**

4. **For some, at least temporary restraint.**

Community

Community members have needs arising from crime, and they have roles to play. Restorative justice advocates such as Judge Barry Stuart and Kay Pranis argue that when the state takes over in our name, it undermines our sense of community.[3] Communities are impacted by crime, and in many cases should be considered stakeholders as secondary victims. Community members have important roles to play and may also have responsibilities to victims, to offenders, and to themselves.

When a community becomes involved in a case, it can initiate a forum to work at these matters, while strengthening the community itself. This topic, too, is a large one. The following list suggests some areas of concern:

Communities need from justice:

1. **Attention to their concerns as victims,**

2. **Opportunities to build a sense of community and mutual accountability,**

3. **Encouragement to take on their obligations for the welfare of their members, including victims and offenders, and to foster the conditions that promote healthy communities.**

Much more could be—and has been—written about who has a stake in a crime and about their needs and roles. However, the basic concerns about the needs and roles of victims, offenders, and community members outlined above continue to provide the focus for both the theory and practice of restorative justice.

> **Restorative justice focuses on needs more than deserts.**

In short, the legal or criminal justice system centers around offenders and deserts—making sure offenders get what they *deserve*. Restorative justice is more focused on *needs*: those of victims, of communities, of offenders.

2.
Restorative
Principles

R estorative justice is based upon an old, common-sense understanding of wrongdoing. Although it would be expressed differently in different cultures, this approach is probably common to most traditional societies. For those of us from a European background, it is the way many of our ancestors (and perhaps even our parents) understood wrongdoing.

- **Crime is a violation of people and of interpersonal relationships.**
- **Violations create obligations.**
- **The central obligation is to put right the wrongs.**

Underlying this understanding of wrongdoing is an assumption about society: we are all interconnected. In the Hebrew scriptures, this is embedded in the concept of shalom, the vision of living in a sense of "all-rightness" with each other, with the creator, and with the environment. Many cultures have a word that represents this notion of the centrality of relationships: for the Maori, it is communicated by *whakapapa*; for the Navajo, *hozho*; for many Africans, the Bantu word *ubuntu*. Although the specific meanings of these words vary, they communicate a similar message: all things are connected to each other in a web of relationships.

The problem of crime, in this worldview, is that it represents a wound in the community, a tear in the web of relationships. Crime represents damaged relationships. In fact, damaged relationships are both a *cause* and an *effect* of crime. Many traditions have a saying that the harm of one is the harm of all. A harm such as crime ripples out to disrupt the whole web. Moreover, wrongdoing is often a symptom that something is out of balance in the web.

Interrelationships imply mutual obligations and responsibilities. It comes as no surprise, then, that this view of wrongdoing emphasizes the importance of making amends or "putting right." Indeed, making amends for wrongdoing is an obligation. While the initial emphasis may be on the obligations owed by offenders, the focus on interconnectedness opens the possibility that others—especially the larger community—may have obligations as well.

Even more fundamentally, this view of wrongdoing implies a concern for healing of those involved—victims, but also offenders and communities.

How does this understanding compare or contrast with the "legal" or criminal justice understanding of crime?

The differences in these two approaches might be boiled down to three central questions asked in the search for justice.

In an often quoted passage from Christian and Jewish scripture, the prophet Micah asks the question, "What does the Lord require?" The answer begins with the

Two Different Views —

Criminal Justice	Restorative Justice
• Crime is a violation of the law and the state.	• Crime is a violation of people and relationships.
• Violations create guilt.	• Violations create obligations.
• Justice requires the state to determine blame (guilt) and impose pain (punishment).	• Justice involves victims, offenders, and community members in an effort to put things right.
• *Central focus: offenders getting what they deserve.*	• *Central focus: victim needs and offender responsibility for repairing harm.*

Three Different Questions —

Criminal Justice	Restorative Justice
• What laws have been broken?	• Who has been hurt?
• Who did it?	• What are their needs?
• What do they deserve?	• Whose obligations are these?

phrase, "to do justice." But what does justice require? As we have seen, Western society's answer has focused on making sure offenders get what they deserve. *Restorative justice answers differently, focusing first of all on needs and associated obligations.*

Appendix I (pages 64-69) provides a fuller statement of restorative justice principles and their implications, based directly on the concept of wrongdoing outlined above. For our purposes here, however, the concept of interrelatedness is basic to understanding why needs, roles, and obligations are so essential to restorative justice.

Three pillars of restorative justice

Three central concepts or pillars deserve a closer look: *harms and needs, obligations,* and *engagement.*

1. Restorative justice focuses on **harm.**

Restorative justice understands crime first of all as harm done to people and communities. Our legal system, with its focus on rules and laws, and with its view that the state is the victim, often loses sight of this reality.

Concerned primarily with making sure offenders get what they deserve, the legal system considers victims, at best, a secondary concern of justice. Focusing on harm, on the contrary, implies an inherent concern for victims' needs and roles.

For restorative justice, then, justice begins with a concern for victims and their needs. It seeks to repair

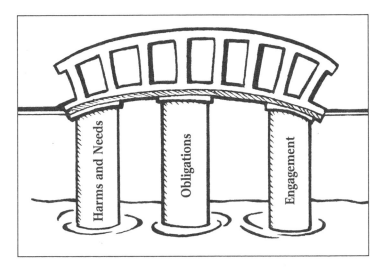

the harm as much as possible, both concretely and symbolically. This victim-oriented approach requires that justice be concerned about victims' needs even when no offender has been identified or apprehended.

While our first concern must be the harm experienced by victims, the focus on harm implies that we also need to be concerned about harm experienced by offenders and communities. This may require us to address the root causes of crime. The goal of restorative justice is to provide an experience of healing for all concerned.

2. *Wrongs or harms result in* obligations.

Therefore, restorative justice emphasizes offender accountability and responsibility.

The legal system defines accountability as making sure offenders are punished. If crime is essentially about harm, however, accountability means offenders must be encouraged to understand that harm. Offenders must begin to comprehend the consequences of their behavior. Moreover, it means they have a responsibility to make things right as much as possible, both concretely and symbolically.

As we shall see, the first obligation is the offender's, but the community and society have obligations as well.

3. *Restorative justice promotes* engagement or participation.

The principle of engagement suggests that the primary parties affected by crime—victims, offenders, members of the community—are given significant roles in the justice process. These "stakeholders" need to be given information about each other and to be involved in deciding what justice requires in this case.

In some cases, this may mean actual dialogue between these parties, as happens in victim offender conferences. They would share their stories and come to a consensus about what should be done. In other cases, it may involve indirect exchanges, the use of surrogates, or other forms of involvement.

The principle of engagement implies involvement of an enlarged circle of parties as compared to the traditional justice process.

So restorative justice is constructed upon three simple elements or pillars: *harms* and related *needs* (of victims, first of all, but also of the communities and the offenders); *obligations* that have resulted from (and given rise to) this harm (the offenders', but also the communities'); and *engagement* of those who have a legitimate interest or stake in the offense and its resolution (victims, offenders, and community members).

Here, in summary, is a skeletal outline of restorative justice. Although it is inadequate by itself, it provides a framework upon which a fuller understanding can be built.

Restorative justice requires, at minimum, that we address victims' harms and needs, hold offenders accountable to put right those harms, and involve victims, offenders, and communities in this process.

The "who" and the "how" are important

Who is involved in the justice process, and how they are involved, is an important part of restorative justice.

Process—the "how"

Our legal system is an adversarial process conducted by professionals who stand in for the offender and the state, refereed by a judge. Outcomes are imposed by an authority—law, judges, juries—who stand outside the essential conflict. Victims, community members, even offenders, rarely participate in this process in any substantial way.

Although restorative justice usually recognizes the need for outside authorities and, in some cases, imposed outcomes, it prefers *processes that are collaborative and inclusive* and, to the extent possible, *outcomes that are mutually agreed upon rather than imposed.*

Restorative justice usually acknowledges a place for the adversarial approach and the role of professionals and recognizes an important role for the state.[1] However, restorative justice emphasizes the importance of participation by those who have a direct stake in the event or offense—that is, those who are involved, impacted by, or who otherwise have a legitimate interest in the offense.

Restorative justice prefers inclusive, collaborative processes and consensual outcomes.

A direct, facilitated, face-to-face encounter—with adequate screening, preparation, and safeguards— is often an ideal forum for the participation of the particular stakeholders. As we shall see shortly, this can take a variety of forms: a meeting between victim and offender, a family group conference, a circle process.

A meeting allows a victim and an offender to put a face to each other, to ask questions of each other directly, to negotiate together how to put things right. It provides an opportunity for victims to tell offenders directly the impact of the offense or to ask questions. It allows offenders to hear and to begin to understand the effects of their behavior. It offers possibilities for acceptance of responsibility and apology. Many victims as well as offenders have found such a meeting to be a powerful and positive experience.

An encounter—direct or indirect—is not always possible, and, in some cases, may not be desirable. In some cultures, a direct encounter may be inappropriate. An indirect encounter, which may be reasonably effective but not offensive, might include a letter, a video exchange, or a person who represents the victim. In all cases, efforts should be made to provide maximum exchange of information between and involvement of the stakeholders.

Stakeholders—the "who"

The key stakeholders, of course, are the immediate victims and offenders. Members of the community may be directly affected and thus should also be considered immediate stakeholders. In addition to this circle, there are others who have varying degrees of stake in the situation. These may include family members, friends, or other "secondary victims"; offenders' families or friends; or other members of the community.

Stakeholders include victims, offenders, and communities of care.

Who is the community?

Controversy has arisen within the restorative justice field about the meaning of community and how actually to involve the community in these processes. The issue is particularly a problem in cultures where traditional communities have eroded, as is true in much of the United States. Furthermore, "community" can be too abstract a concept to be useful. And a community can be guilty of abuses. A discussion of these issues is beyond the scope of this book, but a few observations may be helpful.[2]

In practice, restorative justice has tended to focus on "communities of care" or micro-communities. There are communities of *place*, where people live near and interact with each other, but there are also networks of relationships that are not geographically defined. For restorative justice, the key questions are: 1) who in the community cares about these people or about this offense, and 2) how can we involve them in the process?

It may be helpful to differentiate between "community" and "society." Restorative justice has tended to focus on the micro-communities of place or relationships which are directly affected by an offense but are often neglected by "state justice." However, there are larger concerns and obligations that belong to society beyond those who have a direct stake in a particular event. These include a society's concern for the safety, human rights, and the general well-being of its members. Many argue that the government has an important and legitimate role in looking after such societal concerns.

Restorative justice aims to put things right

We have discussed so far the needs and roles of stakeholders. More needs to be said, however, about the *goals* of justice.

Addressing harm

Central to restorative justice is the idea of making things right or, to use a more active phrase often used in British English, "putting right." As already noted, this implies a responsibility on the part of the offender to, as much as possible, take active steps to repair the harm to the victim (and perhaps the impacted community). In cases such as murder, the harm obviously cannot be repaired; however, symbolic steps, including acknowledgment of responsibility or restitution, can be helpful to victims and are a responsibility of offenders.

Putting right implies reparation or restoration or recovery, but these "re"-words are often inadequate. When a severe wrong has been committed, there is no possibility of repairing the harm or going back to what was before. As Lynn Shiner, the mother of two murdered children, told me, "You build, you create a new life. I have a couple of pieces from my old life that I have fit in."

It is possible that a victim can be helped toward healing when an offender works toward making things right—whether actually or symbolically. Many victims, however, are ambivalent about the term "healing," because of the sense of finality or termination that it connotes. This journey belongs to victims—no one else can do it for them—but an effort to put right can assist in this process, although it can never fully restore.

The obligation to put right is first of all the offender's, but the community may have responsibilities as well—to the victim, but perhaps also to the offender. For offenders to successfully carry out their obligations, they may need support and encouragement from the wider community. Moreover, the community has responsibilities for the situations that are causing or encouraging crime. Ideally, restorative justice processes can provide a catalyst and/or a forum for exploring and assigning these needs, responsibilities, and expectations.

Addressing causes

Putting right requires that we address the harms but also the *causes* of crime. Most victims want this. They want to know that steps are being taken to reduce such harms to themselves and others.

Family group conferences in New Zealand, where restorative justice is the norm, are expected to develop a consensually supported plan that includes elements for both reparation and prevention. These plans must speak to the victims' needs and to offenders' obligations for those needs. But the plan must also address what the offenders need in order to change their behavior.

Offenders have an obligation to address the causes of their behavior, but they usually cannot do this alone. There may be larger obligations beyond those of offenders; for example, the social injustices and other conditions that cause crime or create unsafe conditions. Many times, others in addition to the offenders have responsibilities as well: families, the larger community, society as a whole.

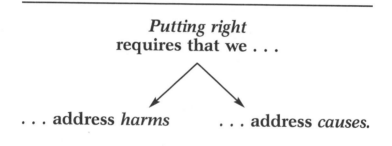

Putting right
requires that we . . .

. . . address *harms*   **. . . address** *causes.*

Offenders as victims

If we are to address harms and causes, we must explore the harms that offenders themselves have experienced.

Studies show that many offenders have indeed been victimized or traumatized in significant ways. Many other offenders perceive themselves to have been victimized. These harms and perceptions of harms may be an important contributing cause of crime. In fact, Harvard professor and former prison psychiatrist James Gilligan has argued that all violence is an effort to achieve justice or to undo injustice.[3] In other words, much crime may be a response to—an effort to undo—a sense of victimization.

A perception of oneself as victim does not absolve responsibility for offending behavior. However, if Gilligan is right, neither can we expect offending behavior to stop without addressing this sense of victimization. In fact, punishment often reinforces the sense of victimization. Sometimes offenders are satisfied when their sense of being victims is simply acknowledged. Sometimes their perception of being victims must be challenged. Sometimes the damage done must be repaired before offenders can be expected to change their behavior.

This is a controversial topic and, understandably, especially difficult for many victims. Too often these reasoned arguments sound like excuses. Moreover, why do some people who are victimized turn to crime and others do not? Nevertheless, I am convinced that any attempt to reduce the causes of offending will require us to explore offenders' experiences of victimization.

Restorative justice balances concern for all.

In this exploration, instead of using the loaded language of victimization, it may be more helpful to speak of "trauma." In her book *Creating Sanctuary*, psychiatrist Sandra Bloom makes the point that unresolved trauma tends to be reenacted. If it is not adequately dealt with, trauma is reenacted in the lives of those who experience the trauma, in their families, even in future generations.[4]

Trauma is a core experience not only of victims, but also of many offenders. Much violence may actually be a reenactment of trauma which was experienced earlier but not responded to adequately. Society tends to respond by delivering more trauma in the form of imprisonment. While the realities of trauma must not be used to excuse, they must be understood, and they must be addressed.

In summary, an effort to put right the wrongs is the hub or core of restorative justice. Putting right has two dimensions: 1. Addressing the harms that have been done, and 2. Addressing the causes of those harms, including the contributing harms.

Since justice should seek to put right, and since victims have been harmed, restorative justice must start with victims.

However, restorative justice is ultimately concerned about the restoration and reintegration of both victims and offenders, in addition to the well-being of the entire community. Restorative justice is about balancing concern for all parties.

Restorative justice encourages outcomes that promote responsibility, reparation, and healing for all.

A restorative lens

Restorative justice seeks to provide an alternate framework or lens for thinking about crime and justice.

Principles

This restorative lens or philosophy has five key principles or actions:

1. Focus on the harms and consequent needs of the victims, as well as the communities' and the offenders';

2. Address the obligations that result from those harms (the obligations of the offenders, as well as the communities' and society's);

3. Use inclusive, collaborative processes;

4. Involve those with a legitimate stake in the situation, including victims, offenders, community members, and society;

5. Seek to put right the wrongs.

We might diagram restorative justice as a wheel. At the hub is the central focus of restorative justice: seeking to put right the wrongs and harms. Each of the spokes represents the four other essential elements outlined above: focusing on harm and needs, addressing obligations, involving stakeholders (victims, offenders, and communities of care), and, to the extent possible, using a collaborative, inclusive process. This needs to be done, of course, in an attitude of respect for all involved.

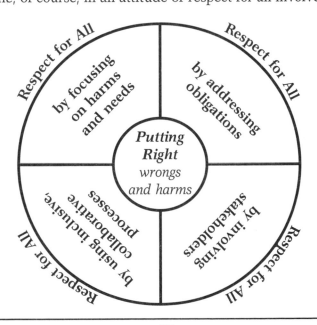

To use an image that is more organic, we might diagram restorative justice as a flower. In the center is the central focus: putting right. Each of the petals represents one of the principles required to succeed in putting right.

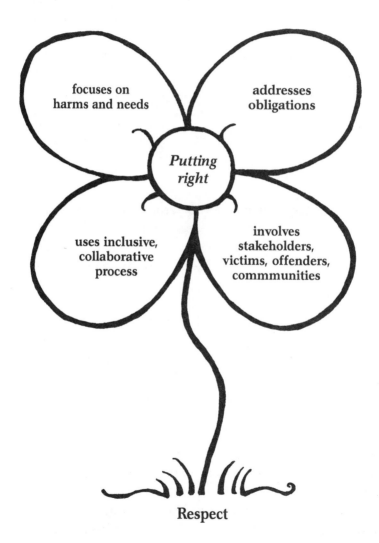

focuses on
harms and needs

addresses
obligations

*Putting
right*

uses inclusive,
collaborative
process

involves
stakeholders,
victims, offenders,
commmunities

Respect

Values

The principles of restorative justice are useful only if they are rooted in a number of underlying values. Too often these values are unstated and taken for granted. However, to apply restorative justice principles in a way that is true to their spirit and intent, we must be explicit about these values. Otherwise, for example, we might use a restoratively-based process but arrive at non-restorative outcomes.

The principles of restorative justice—the hub and the spokes—must be surrounded by a rim of values in order to function properly.

The principles that make up the restorative justice flower must be rooted in values in order to flourish.

Underlying restorative justice is the vision of interconnectedness, which I noted earlier. We are all connected to each other and to the larger world thorough a web of relationships. When this web is disrupted, we are all affected. The primary elements of restorative justice—harm and need, obligation, and participation—derive from this vision.

But this value of interconnectedness must be balanced by an appreciation for particularity. Although we are connected, we are not the same.[5] Particularity appreciates diversity. It respects the individuality and worth of each person. It takes seriously specific contexts and situations.

Justice must acknowledge both our interconnections and our individuality. The value of particularity reminds us that context, culture, and personality are all important.

Much more could and should be said about the values underlying restorative justice. In fact, perhaps one of

restorative justice's greatest attributes is the way it encourages us to explore our values together.

Restorative justice is respect.

Ultimately, however, one basic value is supremely important: re-spect. If I had to put restorative jus-tice into one word, I would choose re-spect: respect for all, even those who are different from us, even those who seem to be our enemies. Respect re-minds us of our interconnectedness but also of our dif-ferences. Respect insists that we balance concern for all parties.

If we pursue justice as respect, we will do justice restoratively.

If we do not respect others, we will not do justice restoratively, no matter how earnestly we adopt the principles.

The value of respect underlies restorative justice principles and must guide and shape their application.

Defining restorative justice

How, then, should restorative justice be defined? Even though there is general agreement on the basic outlines of restorative justice, those in the field have been unable to come to a consensus on its specific meaning. Some of us question the wisdom or useful-ness of such a definition. While we recognize the need for principles and benchmarks, we worry about the ar-rogance and finality of establishing a rigid meaning. With these concerns in mind, I offer this suggestion as a working definition of restorative justice:[6]

Restorative justice is a process to involve,
to the extent possible, those who have a stake
in a specific offense and to collectively
identify and address harms, needs,
and obligations, in order to heal and
put things as right as possible.

The goals of restorative justice

In her excellent handbook, *Restorative Justice: A Vision for Healing and Change,* Susan Sharpe[7] summarized the goals and tasks of restorative justice in this way:

Restorative justice programs aim to:
- put key decisions into the hands of those most affected by crime,
- make justice more healing and, ideally, more transformative, and
- reduce the likelihood of future offenses.

Achieving these goals requires that:
- victims are involved in the process and come out of it satisfied,
- offenders understand how their actions have affected other people and take responsibility for those actions,
- outcomes help to repair the harms done and address the reasons for the offense (specific

plans are tailored to the victim's and the offender's needs), and

- victim and offender both gain a sense of "closure,"[8] and both are reintegrated into the community.

Guiding questions of restorative justice

Ultimately, restorative justice boils down to a set of questions which we need to ask when a wrong occurs. These guiding questions are, in fact, the essence of restorative justice.

Guiding Questions of Restorative Justice

1. Who has been hurt?

2. What are their needs?

3. Whose obligations are these?

4. Who has a stake in this situation?

5. What is the appropriate process to involve stakeholders in an effort to put things right?

If we think of restorative justice as a particular program, or set of programs, we soon find it difficult to apply those programs to a broad variety of situations. For example, the forms of victim-offender conferencing being used for "ordinary" crimes may have little direct application in cases of mass, societal violence. Or, without careful safeguards, restorative justice models of practice may be downright dangerous if applied to situations like domestic violence.

If we instead employ the guiding questions that shape restorative justice, we find restorative justice to be applicable to a wide range of situations. The guiding questions of restorative justice can help us to reframe issues, to think beyond the confines that legal justice has created for society.

These guiding questions are causing some defense attorneys in the U.S. to rethink their roles and obligations in death penalty cases. "Defense-based victim outreach" is emerging as an effort to incorporate survivors' needs and concerns in the trials and their outcomes by giving survivors access to the defense, as well as the prosecution. This approach also seeks to encourage defendants to take appropriate responsibility in these cases. A number of plea agreements have been reached which were based on victims' needs and which allowed offenders to accept responsibility.

In another example, victim advocates are deeply concerned about the dangers of victim-offender encounters in situations of domestic violence. These concerns are legitimate; there are profound dangers in an encounter where a pattern of violence continues or where cases are not being carefully monitored by people trained in domestic violence. Some would argue that encounters are never appropriate. Others, including some victims of domestic violence, argue that encounters are important and powerful in the right situations and with appropriate safeguards.

But whether or not encounters are appropriate in domestic violence, the guiding questions of restorative justice can help us sort out what needs to be done without getting stuck in—and limited to—the question, What does the offender deserve? When faced with a new situation or application, I often turn to these questions as a guide.

The guiding questions of restorative justice may, in fact, be viewed as restorative justice in a nutshell.

Signposts of restorative justice

As we begin to think of practical applications of restorative justice, another guide is provided by the following ten principles or signposts. These principles can be of use in designing or evaluating programs. Like the guiding questions, they may be useful in crafting responses to specific cases or situations.

Signposts of Restorative Justice

1. **Focus on the harms of crime rather than the rules that have been broken.**

2. **Show equal concern and commitment to victims and offenders, involving both in the process of justice.**

3. **Work toward the restoration of victims, empowering them and responding to their needs as they see them.**

4. **Support offenders, while encouraging them to understand, accept, and carry out their obligations.**

5. **Recognize that while obligations may be difficult for offenders, those obligations should not be intended as harms, and they must be achievable.**

6. Provide opportunities for dialogue, direct or indirect, between victim and offender as appropriate.

7. Find meaningful ways to involved the community and to respond to the community bases of crime.

8. Encourage collaboration and reintegration of both victims and offenders, rather than coercion and isolation.

9. Give attention to the unintended consequences of your actions and program.

10. Show respect to all parties—victims, offenders, justice colleagues.

— Harry Mika & Howard Zehr[9]

3.
Restorative
Practices

The concept and philosophy of restorative justice emerged during the 1970s and '80s in the United States and Canada in conjunction with a practice that was then called the Victim Offender Reconciliation Program (VORP). Since then VORP has been modified, new forms of practice have appeared, and older programs have been reshaped and renamed "restorative." What are the main approaches or practices currently being used within the Western criminal justice field? Be aware that the applications in the criminal justice arena that I cite here are by no means the whole picture.

Schools have become an important place for restorative practices. While there are some similarities to restorative justice programs for criminal cases, the approaches used in an educational setting must necessarily be shaped to fit that context.

Restorative approaches are also being adapted to the workplace and to larger community issues and processes. Again, there are similarities to the models outlined below, but there are also important differences. And while the discussion is still often more theoretical than practical, restorative justice has become part of the conversation about how to do justice after large-scale, societal conflicts and wrongdoing.

For those who come from societies closer in time and culture to traditional ways—in Africa, for example, or in North American indigenous communities—restorative justice often serves as a catalyst to reevaluate, resurrect, legitimate, and adapt older, customary approaches. During colonization, the Western legal model often condemned and repressed traditional forms of justice that, although not perfect, were highly functional for those societies.

Restorative justice can provide a conceptual framework to affirm and legitimate what was good about those traditions and, in some cases, develop adapted models that can operate within the realities of the modern legal system. In fact, two of the most important forms of restorative justice—family group conferences and peacemaking circles—are adaptations (but not replications) of these traditional ways.

Restorative justice is also providing a concrete way to think about justice within the theory and practice of conflict transformation and peacebuilding. Most conflicts revolve around, or at least involve, a sense of injustice. Although the field of conflict resolution or conflict transformation has acknowledged this somewhat, the concept and practice of justice in this area has been fairly vague. The principles of restorative justice can provide a concrete framework for addressing justice issues within a conflict.

For example, after taking a restorative justice course in the Conflict Transformation Program at Eastern Mennonite University (Harrisonburg, Virginia), several African practitioners returned to Ghana to continue working with a protracted conflict there. Drawing upon the restorative justice framework, they were able for the first time to address the justice issues in the conflict, using their traditional community justice process. As a result, the peacemaking effort came unstuck and began to move forward.

The restorative justice field is becoming too diverse to capture it in any simple classification. The following, however, is an attempt to provide a brief overview of some of its emerging practices within the Western criminal justice arena.

Core approaches often involve an encounter

Three distinct models have tended to dominate the practice of restorative justice: victim offender conferences, family group conferences, and circle approaches. Increasingly, however, these models are being blended. Family group conferences may utilize a circle, and new forms with elements of each are being developed for certain circumstances. In some cases, several models may be used in a single case or situation. A victim offender encounter may be held prior to and in preparation for a sentencing circle, for example.

All of these models have important elements in common, however. Because of their similarities, they are sometimes grouped together as different forms of restorative conferences.

Each of these models involves an encounter between key stakeholders—victim and offender at minimum, and perhaps other community and justice people as well. Sometimes, if an encounter between a "matched" victim and offender (the particular victim of a particular offender) is impossible or inappropriate, representatives or surrogates may be used. Sometimes letters or videos are used in preparation for, or in place of a direct meeting. All of these models, however, involve some form of encounter, with a preference for face-to-face meetings.

These encounters are led by facilitators who oversee and guide the process, balancing concern for all the parties involved. Unlike arbitrators, conference or circle facilitators do not impose settlements. Each model allows an opportunity for participants to explore facts, feelings, and resolutions. They are encouraged to tell their stories, to ask questions, to express their feelings, and to work toward mutually acceptable outcomes.

Ron Claassen, a longtime restorative justice practitioner, puts it like this. To resolve any type of wrongdoing, three things have to happen:

1. The wrong or injustice must be acknowledged.
2. Equity needs to be restored.
3. Future intentions need to be addressed.[1]

An encounter provides an opportunity for the wrongdoing to be articulated by victims and acknowledged by the offenders. Outcomes such as restitution or apology help to even the score; that is, to restore the equity.

Questions about the future usually need to be discussed: Will the offender do this again? How do we live together in the same community? How do we move ahead with life? All restorative conferencing models provide for such questions to be addressed through a facilitated encounter.

In each of these models, victim participation must be entirely voluntary. In each, there is a prerequisite that the offender acknowledge, at least to some extent, his or her responsibility. Normally, conferences are not held if the offender denies guilt or responsibility. Efforts are made to maximize the offender's *voluntary* participation as well. Certainly conferences should not be held if the offender is unwilling. In reality, there is often some pressure on the offender to choose between lesser evils. In interviews, offenders often suggest that it is difficult and frightening to face the ones they have harmed. Indeed, most of us would try to avoid such obligations if we could.

With the exception of the New Zealand family group conferences, the models described below are usually used on a discretionary, referral basis. For lesser offenses, referrals sometimes come from the community, perhaps from a school or religious institution. Occasionally, referrals are generated by the parties themselves.

Most referrals, however, come from within the justice system with the exact referral point varying with the case and the community. Cases may be referred by the police, by the prosecutor, by probation, by the court, even by prisons. In the case of a court referral, it may be after adjudication but before sentencing. In such instances the judge takes the outcome of the conference into account in the sentence. In some cases or jurisdictions the judge orders restitution and asks that the amount be established through a restorative conference. The agreement then becomes part of the sentence and/or the probation order.

Current programs for victim offender encounters in cases of severe violence are often outside the formal justice system and are designed to be initiated by the parties themselves, most commonly by victims.

Models differ in the "who" and the "how"

While similar in basic outline, the models for restorative justice practices differ in the number and category of participants and, in some cases, the style of facilitation.

Victim Offender Conferences

Victim offender conferences (VOC) primarily involve victims and offenders. Upon referral, victims and offenders are worked with individually. Then, upon their agreement to proceed, they are brought together in a meeting or conference. The meeting is put together and led by a trained facilitator who guides the process in a balanced manner.

A signed restitution agreement is often an outcome, although this is less likely to be true in cases of severe violence. Family members of victims or offenders may participate, but they are usually seen as having secondary, supporting roles. Persons representing the community may be involved as facilitators and/or program overseers, but they do not usually participate in meetings.

Family Group Conferences

Family group conferences (FGC) enlarge the circle of primary participants to include family members or other individuals significant to the parties directly involved. Because this model has tended to focus on supporting offenders in taking responsibility and changing their behavior, the offender's family and/or other relevant people from the community are especially important. However, the victim's family is invited as well. In some circumstances, and especially when the FGC is empowered to affect the legal outcome of the case, a justice person such as a police officer may be present.

Two basic forms of family group conferences have gained prominence. One model that has received considerable attention in North America was initially developed by police in Australia, based in part on ideas from New Zealand. Often this approach has used a standardized, "scripted," model of facilitation. Facilitators may be authority figures such as specially trained police officers. This tradition or approach has given special attention to the dynamics of shame and actively works to use shame in a positive way.

The older model of FGCs, and the one with which I am more familiar, originated in New Zealand, and today provides the norm for juvenile justice in that country. Because this model is less well-known than Victim Offender Conferences (VOCs) or circles (see page 50), at least in the United States, I will describe it somewhat more thoroughly than the others.

Responding to a crisis in the welfare and justice system for juveniles, and criticized by the indigenous Maori population for utilizing an imposed, alien, colonial system, New Zealand revolutionized its juvenile justice system in 1989. While the court system remains as a backup, the standard response to most serious juvenile crime in New Zealand today is an FGC.[2] Consequently, family group conferences can be seen as both a system of justice and as a mode of encounter in New Zealand.

Conferences are put together and facilitated by paid social services personnel called Youth Justice Coordinators. It is their job to help families determine who should be present and to design the process that will be appropriate for them. One of the goals of the process is to be culturally appropriate, and the form of the conference is supposed to be adapted to the needs and cultures of the victims and families involved.

This is not a scripted model of facilitation. While there is often a common overall progression in the conferences, each is adapted to the needs of its particular parties. An element common to most conferences is a family caucus sometime during the conference. Here the offender and the offender's family retire to another room to discuss what has happened and to develop a proposal to bring back to the victim and the rest of the conference.

Like the mediator in a VOC, the coordinator of a FGC must seek to be impartial, balancing the concerns and interests of both sides. However, he or she is charged with making sure a plan is developed that addresses causes as well as reparation, that holds the offender adequately accountable, and that is realistic.

While the community is not explicitly included, these conferences are more inclusive than VOCs. Family members of the offender are an essential part and play very important roles—indeed, this is seen as a family empowerment model. Victims may bring family members or victim advocates. A special attorney or youth advocate may be present, and other caregivers may be as well. In addition, since the police play the role of prosecutors in New Zealand, they must be represented.

Family group conferences, New-Zealand style, are not designed simply to allow for the expression of facts and feelings and to develop restitution agreements. Because they normally take the place of a court, they are charged with developing the entire plan for the offender that, in addition to reparations, includes elements of prevention and sometimes punishment. Even the actual charges may be negotiated in this meeting. Interestingly, the plan is intended to be the consensus of everyone in the conference. The victim, the offender, or the police can each block an outcome if one of them is unsatisfied.

Family group conferences, then, enlarge the circle of participants to include family members or other significant people, and perhaps justice officials as well. At least in the New-Zealand form, a conference may involve a family caucus and the facilitator may have an enlarged role and perhaps a less "neutral" role compared to the VOC facilitator. FGCs, sometimes called community or accountability conferences, are being used experimentally and adapted in a number of countries.

Circles

Circle approaches emerged initially from First Nation communities in Canada. Judge Barry Stuart, in whose court a circle was first acknowledged in a legal ruling, has chosen the term Peacemaking Circles to describe this form. Today, circles are being used for many purposes. In addition to sentencing circles, in-tended to determine sentences in criminal cases, there are healing circles (sometimes used as preparation for sentencing circles), circles to deal with workplace conflicts, even circles designed as forms of community dialogue.

In a circle process, participants arrange themselves in a circle. They pass a "talking piece" around the circle to assure that each person speaks, one at a time, in the order in which each is seated in the circle.

A set of values, or even a philosophy, is often articulated as part of the process—values that emphasize respect, the value of each participant, integrity, the importance of speaking from the heart, and so on.

One or two "circle keepers" serve as facilitators of the circle. In indigenous communities, elders play an important role in leading the circle or in offering advice and insight.

Circles consciously enlarge the circle of participants. Victims, offenders, family members, sometimes justice officials, are included, but community members are essential participants as well. Sometimes these community members are invited because of their connection to or interest in the specific offense or the victim and/or offender; sometimes they are part of an ongoing circle of volunteers from the community.

Because the community is involved, discussions within the circle are often more wide-ranging than in other restorative justice models. Participants may address situations in the community that are giving rise to the offense, the support needs of victims and offenders, the obligations that the community might have, community norms, or other related community issues.

Although circles initially emerged from small, homogeneous communities, they are today being used in a variety of communities, including large urban areas, and for a variety of situations beside criminal cases.

This is not the place to discuss the many forms or the relative merits of each restorative justice model. What should be noted here is that all of the above are forms of encounter. They can be differentiated, however, by the numbers and categories of stakeholders who are included and by their somewhat different styles of facilitation. Again, these forms are increasingly being blended so that the differences among them seem less significant than before.

Please note that not all restorative approaches involve a direct encounter, and not all needs can be met through an encounter. While victims have some needs that involve the offender, they also have needs that do not. Similarly, offenders have needs and obligations that have nothing to do with the victim. Thus the following typology includes both encounter and non-encounter programs.

Models differ in their goals

Another way to understand the differences between these various approaches is to examine their goals. These can be placed in three categories.

Alternative or diversionary programs

These programs usually aim to divert cases from, or provide an alternative to, some part of the criminal justice process or sentencing. Prosecutors may make a referral, deferring prosecution and ultimately dropping it if the case is satisfactorily settled. A judge may refer a case to a restorative conference to sort out elements of the sentence, such as restitution. In some circle processes, the prosecutor and judge may join the community in a circle designed to develop a sentence tailored to the needs of the victim, offender, and community. In Batavia, New York, a long-standing restorative justice program works first with victims of severe crime, then with offenders, to develop alternative pleas, sentences, and even sometimes bail agreements. In New Zealand, of course, conferences are the norm and courts are the alternative.

Healing or therapeutic programs

Increasingly, restorative programs, such as conferences, are being developed for the most severe kinds of crimes—violent assault, even rape and murder. Often the offender in these situations is in prison. In such encounter programs, involvement is not usually designed to impact the outcome of the case. Often, in fact, offenders explicitly agree not to use participation in this process as part of a parole or clemency appeal. With appropriate preparation and structure, such encounters have been found to be powerful, positive experiences for both victims and offenders, regardless of who initiates them.

Not all programs in this category involve direct encounters between "matched" victims and offenders. Rather, some programs function as a form of victim-oriented offender rehabilitation. As part of the treatment process, offenders are encouraged to understand and take responsibility for what they have done. Victim-impact panels, where groups of victims are given an opportunity to tell their stories to offenders, may be part of this process. Other programs offer multiple-session, in-prison seminars that bring victims, offenders, and sometimes community members together to explore a variety of topics and issues, for the benefit of all involved.

Transitional programs

A relatively new arena of restorative programming has to do with offender transitions after prison. In both halfway houses and in prisons, programs are being designed around victim harm and offender accountability in order to help both victims and offenders as the offender returns to the community.

One of the most interesting models is the Circles of Support and Accountability (CSA) developed in Canada to work with released sex offenders. In much of the U.S. and Canada, sex offenders who serve out their sentences are released into communities with little support for the offender and with great fear from the community and victims. These offenders (hopefully, ex-offenders) are often ostracized by the communities that know them best, so they move on to other communities. Given this, their rates of recidivism can be high.

Circles of Support and Accountability gather a circle of people—ex-offenders, community members, even victims of similar offenses—not only to support these offenders, but to hold them accountable. Initially the interaction is intense with daily check-ins and strict guidelines for what the person can do and where the person can go. Working with these ex-offenders to take responsibility for their behavior, while putting necessary support in place, these circles have been successful in reintegrating ex-offenders while allaying community fears.

A restorative continuum

Most of the encounter models described above would be considered fully restorative. They meet all of the criteria laid out in the guidelines for restorative justice that I outlined earlier. But what about other approaches that claim to be restorative? Are there other options within the restorative framework?

It is important to view restorative justice models along a continuum, from fully restorative to not restorative, with several points or categories in between.[3]

Degrees of restorative justice practices: a continuum

fully restorative — *mostly restorative* — *partially restorative* — *potentially restorative* — *pseudo- or non-restorative*

Six key questions help to analyze both the effectiveness and the extent of restorative justice models for particular situations:

1. Does the model address harms, needs, and causes?
2. Is it adequately victim-oriented?
3. Are offenders encouraged to take responsibility?
4. Are all relevant stakeholders involved?
5. Is there an opportunity for dialogue and participatory decision-making?
6. Is the model respectful to all parties?

While conferencing or encounter programs may be fully restorative, there are situations in which these models do not fully—or even partially—apply. What about victims in cases where offenders are not apprehended or offenders are unwilling to take responsibility?

In a restorative system, services would start immediately after a crime to address victim needs and to involve the victim, regardless of whether an offender is apprehended. Thus victim assistance, while it cannot be seen as fully restorative, is an important component of a restorative system and should be seen at least as partially restorative.

Victim impact panels, without matching victims and offenders from a specific case, allow victims to tell their stories and encourage offenders to understand what they have done. These are an important part of a restorative approach and can be seen as partly or mostly restorative.

Similarly, what happens when an offender is willing to take steps to understand and to take responsibility, but the victim is unavailable or unwilling? A few programs for such circumstances have been developed (such as offering opportunities to learn from victims and to do symbolic acts of restitution), but more should be available. While perhaps not fully restorative, these programs play an essential role in the overall system of justice.

Do offender treatment or rehabilitation programs qualify as restorative justice practices? Offender treatment can be seen as a part of prevention and, along with offender reintegration, has some kinship with restorative justice. However, as conventionally practiced, many efforts at treatment or rehabilitation offer little that is explicitly restorative. They could, however, function restoratively, and some do, by organizing treatment around offenders understanding and taking responsibility for harm and, in addition, giving as much attention as possible to victims' needs.

Depending on how it is done, offender treatment may fall into the "potentially," or "mostly" categories.

Similarly, offender advocacy, prisoner re-entry programs, or religious teaching in prison are in themselves not restorative; however, they may play an important role in a restorative system, especially if they are reshaped to include a restorative framework.

In my view, community service falls into the "potentially restorative" category. As currently practiced, community service is at best an alternative form of punishment, not restorative justice. In New Zealand, however, community service often is part of the outcome of a family group conference. All in the group have participated in developing the plan, the work is connected to the offense as much as possible, and within the plan are specifics about how the community and family will support and monitor the agreement. Here it has potential for being seen as repayment to or a contribution to the community, mutually agreed upon by all participants. With this kind of re-framing, community service may have an important place in a restorative approach.

Then there is the "pseudo-" or "non-restorative" category. "Restorative" has become such a popular term that many acts and efforts are being labeled "restorative," but in fact they are not. Some of these might be rescued. Others cannot. The death penalty, which causes additional and irreparable harm, is one of the latter.

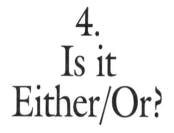

4.
Is it
Either/Or?

In my earlier writings, I often drew a sharp contrast between the retributive framework of the legal or criminal justice system and a more restorative approach to justice. More recently, however, I have come to believe that this polarization may be somewhat misleading. Although charts that highlight contrasting characteristics illuminate some important elements differentiating the two approaches, they also mislead and hide important similarities and areas of collaboration.

Retributive justice vs. restorative justice?

For example, philosopher of law Conrad Brunk has argued that on the theoretical or philosophical level, retribution and restoration are not the polar opposites that we often assume.[1] In fact, they have much in common. A primary goal of both retributive theory and restorative theory is to vindicate through reciprocity, by evening the score. Where they differ is in what each suggests will effectively right the balance.

Both retributive and restorative theories of justice acknowledge a basic moral intuition that a balance has been thrown off by a wrongdoing. Consequently, the victim deserves something and the offender owes something. Both approaches argue that there must be a proportional relationship between the act and the response. They differ, however, on the currency that will fulfill the obligations and right the balance.

Retributive theory believes that pain will vindicate, but in practice that is often counterproductive for both victim and offender. Restorative justice theory, on the other hand, argues that what truly vindicates is acknowledgment of victims' harms and needs, combined with an active effort to encourage offenders to take responsibility, make right the wrongs, and address the causes of their behavior. By addressing this need for vindication in a positive way, restorative justice has the potential to affirm both victim and offender and to help them transform their lives.

Criminal justice vs. restorative justice?

Restorative justice advocates dream of a day when justice is fully restorative, but whether this is realistic is debatable, at least in the immediate future. More attainable, perhaps, is a time when restorative justice is the norm, while some form of the legal or criminal justice system provides the backup or alternative. Possible, perhaps, is a time when all our approaches to justice will be restoratively oriented.

Society must have a system to sort out the "truth" as best it can when people deny responsibility. Some cases are simply too difficult or horrendous to be worked out by those with a direct stake in the offense. We must have a process that gives attention to those societal needs and obligations that go beyond the ones held by the immediate stakeholders. We also must not lose those qualities which the legal system at its best represents: the rule of law, due process, a deep regard for human rights, the orderly development of law.

Real world justice might also best be viewed as a continuum. On the one end is the Western legal or criminal justice system model. Its strengths—such as the encouragement of human rights—are substantial. Yet it has some glaring weaknesses. At the other end is the restorative alternative. It, too, has important strengths. It, too, has limits, at least as it is currently conceived and practiced.

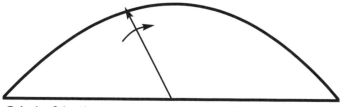

Criminal justice   *Restorative justice*

A realistic goal, perhaps, is to move as far as we can toward a process that is restorative. In some cases or situations, we may not be able to move very far. In others, we may achieve processes and outcomes that are truly restorative. In between will be many cases and situations where both systems must be utilized, and justice is only partly restorative.

Meanwhile, we can dream of a day when this particular continuum is no longer relevant because its both ends will rest on a restorative foundation.

Restorative justice is a river

Some years ago, while living in Pennsylvania, my wife and I set out to find the source of the Susquehanna River that flows through that state. We followed one of its two branches until we arrived behind a farmer's barn and found a rusty pipe sticking out of a hill. Fed by a spring, the water fell from the pipe into a bathtub that served as a watering trough for cattle. It spilled over the bathtub, spread out along the ground, then formed the stream that eventually became a mighty river.

It is, of course, debatable whether this particular spring is *the* source. There are other springs in the vicinity that could compete for that honor. And, of course, this stream would not be a river if it were not fed by hundreds of other streams. Nevertheless, this river and this spring have become my metaphor for the restorative justice movement.

The contemporary field of restorative justice started as a tiny trickle in the 1980s, an effort by a handful of people dreaming of doing justice differently. It originated in practice and in experimentation rather than in abstractions. The theory, the concept, came later. But while the immediate sources of the modern restorative justice stream are recent, both concept and practice draw upon traditions as deep as human history and as wide as the world community.

For some time the restorative justice stream was driven underground by our modern legal systems. In the last quarter century, however, that stream has resurfaced, growing into a widening river. Restorative justice today is acknowledged worldwide by governments and communities concerned about crime. Thousands of people around the globe bring their experience and expertise to the river. This river, like all rivers, exists because it is being fed by numerous tributaries flowing in from around the world.

Some of the feeder streams are practical programs, such as those being implemented in many countries throughout the globe. The river is also being fed by a variety of indigenous traditions and current adaptations which draw upon those traditions: family group conferences adapted from Maori traditions in New Zealand, for example; sentencing circles from aboriginal communities in the Canadian north; Navajo peacemaking courts; African customary law; or the Afghani practice of *jirga*. The field of mediation and conflict resolution feeds into that river, as do the victims-rights movements, and alternatives-to-prison movements of the past decades. A variety of religious traditions flow into this river.

While the experiments, practices, and customs from many communities and cultures are instructive, none can or should be copied and simply plugged into communities or societies. Rather, they should be viewed as examples of how different communities and societies found their own appropriate ways to express justice as a response to wrongdoing. These approaches may give us inspiration and a place to begin. While these examples and traditions may not provide blueprints, they may serve as catalysts for forming ideas and directions.

This context-oriented approach to justice reminds us that true justice emerges from conversation and takes into account local needs and traditions. This is one of the reasons why we must be very cautions about top-down strategies for implementing restorative justice.

The argument presented here is quite simple: justice will not be served if we maintain our exclusive focus on the questions that drive our current justice systems: What laws have been broken? Who did it? What do they deserve?

True justice requires, instead, that we ask questions such as these: Who has been hurt? What do they need? Whose obligations and responsibilities are these? Who has a stake in this situation? What is the process that can involve the stakeholders in finding a solution? Restorative justice requires us to change not just our lenses but our questions.

Above all, restorative justice is an invitation to join in conversation so that we may support and learn from each other. It is a reminder that all of us are indeed interconnected.

Fundamental Principles of Restorative Justice

Howard Zehr and Harry Mika [1]

1.0 Crime is fundamentally a violation of people and interpersonal relationships.

1.1 Victims and the community have been harmed and are in need of restoration.

1.1.1 The primary victims are those most directly affected by the offense, but others, such as family members of victims and offenders, witnesses, and members of the affected community, are also victims.

1.1.2 The relationships affected (and reflected) by crime must be addressed.

1.1.3 Restoration is a continuum of responses to the range of needs and harms experienced by victims, offenders, and the community.

1.2 Victims, offenders, and the affected communities are the key stakeholders in justice.

1.2.1 A restorative justice process maximizes the input and participation of these parties—but especially primary victims as well as offenders—in the search for restoration, healing, responsibility, and prevention.

1.2.2 The roles of these parties will vary according to the nature of the offense, as well as the capacities and preferences of the parties.

1.2.3 The state has circumscribed roles, such as investigating facts, facilitating processes, and ensuring safety, but the state is not a primary victim.

2.0 Violations create obligations and liabilities.

2.1 Offenders' obligations are to make things right as much as possible.

2.1.1 Since the primary obligation is to victims, a restorative justice process empowers victims to effectively participate in defining obligations.

2.1.2 Offenders are provided opportunities and encouragement to understand the harm they have caused to victims and the community and to develop plans for taking appropriate responsibility.

2.1.3 Voluntary participation by offenders is maximized; coercion and exclusion are minimized. However, offenders may be required to accept their obligations if they do not do so voluntarily.

2.1.4 Obligations that follow from the harm inflicted by crime should be related to making things right.

2.1.5 Obligations may be experienced as difficult, even painful, but are not intended as pain, vengeance, or revenge.

2.1.6 Obligations to victims, such as restitution, take priority over other sanctions and obligations to the state, such as fines.

2.1.7 Offenders have an obligation to be active participants in addressing their own needs.

2.2 *The community's obligations are to victims and to offenders and for the general welfare of its members.*

2.2.1 The community has a responsibility to support and help victims of crime to meet their needs.

2.2.2 The community bears a responsibility for the welfare of its members and the social conditions and relationships which promote both crime and community peace.

2.2.3 The community has responsibilities to support efforts to integrate offenders into the community, to be actively involved in the definitions of offender obligations, and to ensure opportunities for offenders to make amends.

3.0 Restorative justice seeks to heal and put right the wrongs.

3.1 The needs of victims for information, validation, vindication, restitution, testimony, safety, and support are the starting points of justice.

3.1.1 The safety of victims is an immediate priority.

3.1.2 The justice process provides a framework that promotes the work of recovery and healing that is ultimately the domain of the individual victim.

3.1.3 Victims are empowered by maximizing their input and participation in determining needs and outcomes.

3.1.4 Offenders are involved in repair of the harm insofar as possible.

3.2 The process of justice maximizes opportunities for exchange of information, participation, dialogue, and mutual consent between victim and offender.

3.2.1 Face-to-face encounters are appropriate for some instances, while alternative forms of exchange are more appropriate in others.

3.2.2 Victims have the principal role in defining and directing the terms and conditions of the exchange.

3.2.3 Mutual agreement takes precedence over imposed outcomes.

3.2.4 Opportunities are provided for remorse, forgiveness, and reconciliation.

3.3 Offenders' needs and competencies are addressed.

3.3.1 Recognizing that offenders themselves have often been harmed, healing and integration of offenders into the community are emphasized.

3.3.2 Offenders are supported and treated respectfully in the justice process.

3.3.3 Removal from the community and severe restriction of offenders is limited to the minimum necessary.

3.3.4 Justice values personal change above compliant behavior.

3.4 The justice process belongs to the community.

3.4.1 Community members are actively involved in doing justice.

3.4.2 The justice process draws from community resources and, in turn, contributes to the building and strengthening of community.

3.4.3 The justice process attempts to promote changes in the community to both prevent similar harms from happening to others, and to foster early intervention to address the needs of victims and the accountability of offenders.

3.5 Justice is mindful of the outcomes, intended and unintended, of its responses to crime and victimization.

3.5.1 Justice monitors and encourages follow-through since healing, recovery, accountability, and change are maximized when agreements are kept.

3.5.2 Fairness is assured, not by uniformity of outcomes, but through provision of necessary support and opportunities to all parties and avoidance of discrimination based on ethnicity, class, and sex.

3.5.3 Outcomes which are predominately deterrent or incapacitative should be implemented as a last resort, involving the least restrictive intervention while seeking restoration of the parties involved.

3.5.4 Unintended consequences such as the co-optation of restorative processes for coercive or punitive ends, undue offender orientation, or the expansion of social control, are resisted.

Endnotes

Chapter 1

[1] Language is often quite problematic here. The terms "victim" and "offender" are often too simplistic and stereotypical. Because this book is directed toward the criminal justice arena, however, and because the alternatives are often awkward, I have nevertheless used that language. Similarly, the term "stakeholder" is problematic; it may in fact originate from white settlers driving their stakes into the ground to mark what was originally Native land.

[2] Shame theory, though controversial, has emerged as an important topic in restorative justice. In his pioneering book, *Crime, Shame, and Reintegration* (Cambridge, U.K., 1989), John Braithwaite argues that shame that stigmatizes pushes people toward crime. Shame may be "reintegrative," however, when it denounces the offense but not the offender, and opportunities are provided for the shame to be removed or transformed.

[3] See, for example, their chapters in *Restorative Community Justice: Repairing Harm and Transforming Communities* (Anderson, U.S. 2001).

Chapter 2

[1] The role of the state is most contested in situations where minority groups have felt systematically oppressed by the government (e.g., in Northern Ireland), or where the state is viewed as having co-opted restorative justice while implementing it from the top down. The latter has been a particular concern of community and indigenous groups, for example, in New Zealand and Canada.

[2] An overview of this debate may be found in Gerry Johnstone, *Restorative Justice: Ideas, Values, Debates* (Willan, U.K., 2002), 136ff. This book provides a helpful overview and analysis of the debates and critical issues in the field of restorative justice.

[3] James Gilligan, *Violence: Reflections on a National Epidemic* (New York: Random House, 1996).

[4] Sandra Bloom, *Creating Sanctuary: Toward the Evolution of Sane Societies* (Routledge, U.S., 1997).

[5] I am indebted here to Jarem Sawatsky for his important work (as yet unpublished) on the values underlying restorative justice.

[6] This is an adaptation of Tony Marshall's definition: "Restorative Justice is a process whereby all parties with a stake in a specific offense come together to resolve collectively how to deal with the aftermath of the offense and its implications for the future."

[7] Susan Sharpe, *Restorative Justice: A Vision for Healing and Change,* is published by the Mediation and Restorative Justice Centre, #430, 9810-111 St., Edmonton, AB, Canada, T5K 1K1. www.edmontonmediation.com

[8] The word "closure" is often offensive to victims, especially of severe crime. It seems to suggest that all can be put behind and the book closed, and that is not possible. However, the word does imply a sense of being able to move forward, which restorative justice aims to make possible.

[9] These signposts were originally published, in a somewhat different version, as a bookmark by Mennonite Central Committee, Akron, Pennsylvania, in 1997.

Chapter 3

[1] http://www.fresno.edu/pacs/docs/model.shtml

[2] The youth justice system in New Zealand is designed to divert offenders in less serious cases out of the system. This is sometimes done in conjunction with an informal victim offender conference.

[3] See Paul McCold, "Toward a Holistic Vision of Restorative Juvenile Justice: A Reply to the Maximalist Model," in *Contemporary Justice Review,* 2000, Vol. 3(4), 357-414, for a discussion of definitional issues and restorative justice criteria. McCold's view is based on the Marshall definition cited earlier.

Chapter 4

[1] Conrad Brunk, "Restorative Justice and the Philosophical Theories of Criminal Punishment" in *The Spiritual Roots of Restorative Justice,* Michael L. Hadley, editor. (Albany, NY: State University of New York Press, 2001), 31-56.

Appendix I

[1] Howard Zehr and Harry Mika, "Fundamental Principles of Restorative Justice," *The Contemporary Justice Review,* Vol. 1, No. 1 (1998), 47-55.

Selected Readings

General introductions to restorative justice

Cayley, David. *The Expanding Prison: The Crisis in Crime and Punishment and the Search for Alternatives* (House of Anasi Press, Canada, 1998).

Consedine, Jim. *Restorative Justice: Healing the Effects of Crime* (Plowshares, New Zealand, 2nd edition).

Johnstone, Gerry. *Restorative Justice: Ideas, Values, Debates* (Willan Publishing, U.K., 2002).

Ross, Rupert. *Returning to the Teachings: Exploring Aboriginal Justice* (Penguin, Canada, 1996).

Sharpe, Susan. *Restorative Justice: A Vision for Healing and Change* (Mediation & Restorative Justice Centre, Suite 430, 9810 - 111 St., Edmonton, Alberta T5K 1K1, Canada, 1998).

Van Ness, Dan and Karen Heetderks Strong. *Restoring Justice* (Anderson, U.S., 2nd edition, 2001).

Wright, Martin. *Justice for Victims and Offenders* (Waterside Press, U.K., 2nd edition, 1996).

Zehr, Howard. *Changing Lenses: A New Focus for Crime and Justice* (Scottdale, Pennsylvania: Herald Press, 1990/95).

For restorative justice websites and a more extensive bibliography, see http://www.restorativejustice.org.

Related books by Howard Zehr

Doing Life: Reflections of Men and Women Serving Life Sentences (Intercourse, Pennsylvania: Good Books, 1996).

Transcending: Reflections of Crime Victims (Intercourse, Pennsylvania: Good Books, 2001).

About the Author

Howard Zehr has been called the grand-father of restorative justice. He directed the first victim offender conferencing program in the U.S. and is one of the developers of restorative justice as a concept. His book *Changing Lenses: A New Focus for Crime and Justice* is considered a classic in the field. His many other publications include *Doing Life: Reflections of Men and Women Serving Life Sentences* and *Transcending: Reflections of Crime Victims.*

Tammy Krause

Dr. Zehr is co-director of the graduate Center for Justice and Peacebuilding at Eastern Mennonite University (Harrisonburg, Virginia). From this base he also teaches and practices in the field of restorative justice. Zehr received his M.A. from the University of Chicago and his Ph.D. from Rutgers University.

A list of Study Questions to enrich group discussion of this book is available (free of charge) on the Good Books website at www.GoodBooks.com.

METHOD OF PAYMENT

❏ Check or Money Order
*(payable to **Good Books** in U.S. funds)*

❏ Please charge my:
    ❏ MasterCard   ❏ Visa
    ❏ Discover   ❏ American Express

\# _____

exp. date _____

Signature _____

Name _____

Address _____

City _____

State _____

Zip _____

Phone _____

Email _____

SHIP TO: (if different)

Name _____

Address _____

City _____

State _____

Zip _____

Mail order to: **Good Books**
P.O. Box 419 • Intercourse, PA 17534-0419
Call toll-free: 800/762-7171
Fax toll-free: 888/768-3433
Prices subject to change.

The Little Book of Restorative Justice
ORDER FORM

If you would like to order multiple copies of *The Little Book of Restorative Justice* by Howard Zehr for groups you know or are a part of, use this form. (Discounts apply only for more than one copy.)

Photocopy this page as often as you like.

The following discounts apply:

1 copy	$4.95
2-5 copies	$4.45 each (a 10% discount)
6-10 copies	$4.20 each (a 15% discount)
11-20 copies	$3.96 each (a 20% discount)
21-99 copies	$3.45 each (a 30% discount)
100 or more	$2.97 each (a 40% discount)

Free shipping for U.S. orders of 100 or more!

Prices subject to change.

Quantity   *Price*   *Total*

_____ copies of **Restorative Justice**   @ _____ _____

Shipping & Handling
(U.S. orders only: add 10%; $3.95 minimum) _____
For international orders, please call 800/762-7171, ext. 221

PA residents add 6% sales tax _____

TOTAL _____

800/762-7171 • www.GoodBooks.com